Spousal/Partner Visa to the U.K. A comprehensive Guide.

Arthur Crandon LL.B (Hons), M.A.

Spousal/Partner visa to the UK

Copyright Arthur Crandon 2024

All rights reserved. No part of this book may be reproduced, stored in a retrieval system, or transmitted in any form or by any means—electronic, mechanical, photocopying, recording, or otherwise—without the prior written permission of the publisher, except for brief quotations in critical reviews or articles.

This is a work of fiction. Names, characters, places, and incidents are either the product of the author's imagination or used fictitiously. Any resemblance to actual persons, living or dead, events, or locales is entirely coincidental.

ISBN: 9798336410457

Cover design by Lynnie Ceniza
Interior design and formatting by Lynnie Ceniza
Published by Arthur Crandon Publishing
Visit our website: Arthurcrandon.co.uk

DISCLAIMER

The information provided in this book is for general informational purposes only. It does not constitute legal, financial, or professional advice. While every effort has been made to ensure accuracy, the author and publisher assume no responsibility for errors or omissions. Readers should consult with appropriate professionals for specific advice tailored to their individual circumstances.

First Edition: August 2024

Visit Arthurcrandon.co.uk for More Titles

Retirement to the Philippines
K1 Fiance visa to the U.S. – Fast Track
Secrets to buying Condos in the Philippines
Buying Land in the Philippines
Annulment in the Philippines
Breaking free from a bad marriage
Get a visit visa to America First time
Marriage in the Philippines
Get a visit visa to the United Kingdom
Ghosts, Spectres, and folklore in the Philippines
Retiring to Spain – a Comprehensive Guide
Spousal Visa to America
Spousal visa to the United Kingdom

ABOUT THE AUTHOR

Arthur Crandon is a retired lawyer and a prolific writer. Hi is British and grew up in a rural community in Somerset. He has lived in England, Wales, Hong Kong and the Philippines and now spends most of his time in the Philippines with his Visayan wife and their son.

He loves to hear from anyone who has anything to do with the Philippines – you can email him anytime on:

ac@arthurcrandon.co.uk

CONTENTS

1	Determining Eligibility	1
2	The Application	5
3	Documents	11
4	Paying for the Application	17
5	Completing the form	21
6	Biometric Information	25
7	Supporting Documents	29
8	The Interview	35
9	Waiting for a Decision	39
10	Travel to the UK	43

1 DETERMINE ELIGIBILITY

The first and most important thing is to establish your partner's eligibility for the visa. Here are more detailed explanations for each eligibility criterion for a UK spouse or partner visa:

1. Age Requirement

- **Both must be 18 or over**: This ensures that both parties are legally adults and capable of making independent decisions regarding their relationship and residency.

2. Status of the UK Citizen

- **You must be a British citizen or have settled status in the UK**: This means you must either:
    - Be a British citizen.

- Have indefinite leave to remain (ILR) or settled status.

- Have pre-settled status under the EU Settlement Scheme.

- <u>Have refugee status or humanitarian protection in the UK</u>.

3. Intention to Live Together Permanently

- **You must intend to live together permanently in the UK**: This requirement is to ensure that the relationship is genuine and not solely for immigration purposes. Evidence of this intention can include:

  - Joint tenancy agreements or mortgage documents.

  - Correspondence addressed to both partners at the same address.

  - <u>Statements from friends and family confirming your relationship</u>.

4. Proof of Relationship

- **You must be able to prove your relationship**: Depending on your situation, you need to provide specific evidence:

    - **Marriage or Civil Partnership**: A marriage or civil partnership certificate recognized in the UK.

    - **Living Together for at Least 2 Years**: Documents showing you have lived together for at least 2 years, such as joint bank statements, utility bills, or rental agreements.

    - **Fiancé(e) or Proposed Civil Partner**: Proof that you plan to marry or enter into a civil partnership within 6 months of arriving in the UK. <u>This can include wedding plans, venue bookings, or invitations</u>[1].

Additional Requirements

- **Financial Requirement**: You must meet the financial requirement, which usually means having an income of at least £18,600 per year. This amount is currently under review, so be sure to check the latest guidelines. This amount increases if you have children.

- **Knowledge of English**: Your partner must prove they have a good knowledge of English, usually by passing an approved English language test or having an academic qualification taught in English.

Exceptions

- If you cannot meet the financial requirement, you may still be able to apply if:
    - You have a child in the UK who is a British or Irish citizen or has lived in the UK for 7 years and it would be unreasonable for them to leave the UK.

    - It would breach your human rights to stop you from coming to the UK or make you leave.

These details should help clarify the eligibility criteria for a UK spouse or partner visa.

2 THE APPLICATION

Here are more detailed explanations for the financial and English language requirements for a UK spouse or partner visa:

Financial Requirements

Minimum Income Threshold

- **Income Requirement:** You must have a combined income of at least £18,600 per year. This amount increases if you have dependent children:
    - One child: An additional £3,800 per year.
    - Each additional child: An additional £2,400 per year.

- **Sources of Income:** The income can come from various sources, including:

    - **Employment or Self-Employment:** Payslips, tax returns, or business accounts.

    - **Savings:** If your income falls short, you can use savings to meet the requirement. <u>You need at least £16,000 plus 2.5 times the shortfall amount</u>.

    - **Pensions:** Pension statements.

    - **Other Income:** Rental income, dividends, or other investments.

Evidence Required

- **Payslips:** Typically, you need to provide 6 months of payslips.

- **Bank Statements:** Corresponding bank statements showing the income being deposited.

- **Employment Letter:** A letter from your employer confirming your job and salary.
- **Tax Returns:** For self-employed applicants,

recent tax returns and business accounts.

Exemptions

- **If your partner receives certain disability or carer's benefits, you do not need to meet the minimum income requirement**.

Knowledge of English

Proving English Proficiency

Your partner must prove they have a good knowledge of English. This can be done in one of the following ways:

1. **Approved English Language Tes**t:

    - **Test Level:** Your partner must pass at least level A1 on the Common European Framework of Reference for Languages (CEFR) scale for the initial visa application.

    - **Test Providers:** The test must be taken with a Home Office-approved provider. Examples include IELTS for UKVI and Trinity College London.

2. **Academic Qualifications:**

    o **UK Degree:** If your partner has a degree from a UK university, they only need to provide the degree certificate.

    o <u>**Non-UK Degree:** If the degree is from outside the UK, your partner needs a certificate from Ecctis (formerly UK NARIC) to show that the qualification is equivalent to a UK bachelor's degree or higher and was taught in English</u>.

Exemptions

- **Your partner does not need to prove their knowledge of English if they are:**

    o A national of a majority English-speaking country (e.g., USA, Canada, Australia).

    o Over 65 years old.

    o <u>Unable to meet the requirement due to a long-term physical or mental condition</u>.

These details should help clarify the financial and English language requirements for a UK spouse or partner visa.

3 DOCUMENTS

Here are more detailed explanations for each of the required documents for a UK spouse or partner visa:

1. Valid Passport or Travel ID

- **Applicant's Passport**: A valid passport or travel document for your partner. This should be current and have at least one blank page for the visa vignette.

- **Sponsor's Passport**: A copy of your passport or travel document to prove your British citizenship or settled status.

2. Proof of Relationship

- **Marriage or Civil Partnership Certificate**: If you are married or in a civil partnership, provide the official certificate.

- **Evidence of Living Together**: If you are not married but have lived together for at least 2 years, provide documents such as:

    o Joint tenancy agreements or mortgage statements.

    o Utility bills or council tax bills in both names.

    o Joint bank account statements.

    o <u>Correspondence addressed to both partners at the same address over the 2-year period</u>.

    ### 3. Financial Documents

- **Payslips**: Typically, 6 months of payslips from your employment.

- **Bank Statements**: Corresponding bank

statements showing the income being deposited.

- **Employment Letter**: A letter from your employer confirming your job, salary, and length of employment.

- **Self-Employment Documents**: If self-employed, provide recent tax returns, business accounts, and an accountant's letter.

- <u>**Savings**: If using savings to meet the financial requirement, provide bank statements showing the savings have been held for at least 6 months</u>.

4. Proof of Accommodation in the UK

- **Tenancy Agreement or Mortgage Statement**: Proof of where you will live in the UK. This can be a rental agreement, mortgage statement, or a letter from family or friends confirming you can stay with them.

- <u>**Property Inspection Report**: Sometimes required to show that the accommodation</u>

is adequate and not overcrowded.

5. English Language Test Results (if applicable)

- **Approved English Language Test Certificate**: If your partner needs to prove their knowledge of English, provide the test certificate from an approved provider. The test must be at least level A1 on the CEFR scale.

- **Academic Qualifications**: If your partner has a degree taught in English, provide the degree certificate and a certificate from Ecctis (formerly UK NARIC) confirming the qualification is equivalent to a UK degree.

Additional Documents

- **TB Test Certificate**: If your partner is from a country where tuberculosis (TB) testing is required, provide a TB test certificate from an approved clinic.

Previous Immigration Documents: If your

partner has previously been in the UK, provide copies of any previous visas or residence permits.

These details should help you gather all the necessary documents for a UK spouse or partner visa application.

4 PAYING THE APPLICATION FEE.

Application Fee

Applying from Outside the UK

- **Fee**: £1,846 (Subject to review – check at the time of your application.)

- **Payment**: This fee is paid online during the application process. It covers the cost of processing your visa application.

Applying from Inside the UK

- **Fee**: £1,048.

- **Payment**: This fee is also paid online during the application process. It applies to those extending or switching their visa within the UK.

Healthcare Surcharge (Immigration Health Surcharge - IHS)

What is the IHS?

The Immigration Health Surcharge (IHS) is a fee that allows visa holders to access the UK's National Health Service (NHS). It must be paid upfront for the entire duration of the visa.

Cost of the HIS

- **Standard Rate**: £1,035 per year.

- **Discounted Rate**: £776 per year for students, their dependents, and those on the Youth Mobility Scheme.

How to Calculate the HIS

- **Example**: If your visa is valid for 2.5 years, you would pay £1,035 x 2.5 = £2,587.50.

- **Payment**: The IHS is paid online as part of the visa application process. You will receive an IHS reference number, which you need to include in your visa application.

Who Needs to Pay?

- **Most Applicants**: Anyone applying for a visa to stay in the UK for more than 6 months.

- **Exemptions**: Certain visa categories and applicants, such as those applying for indefinite leave to remain, are exempt from paying the IHS.

Additional Information

- **Refunds**: If your visa application is refused, you will receive a refund for the IHS but not the application fee.

- **Payment Confirmation**: Ensure you keep a copy of your payment confirmation and IHS reference number for your records.

These details should help clarify the

application fee and healthcare surcharge for a UK spouse or partner visa.

5 COMPLETING THE APPLICATION FORM

Online Application

- **Website**: <u>The application is completed online through the UK Visas and Immigration (UKVI) website</u>.

- **Account Creation**: You will need to create an account on the UKVI website to start your application.

- **Application Process**: Follow the step-by-step instructions provided on the website. You will be asked to fill in various sections, upload documents, and pay the application fee.

Form VAF4A

- **Purpose**: The VAF4A form is specifically for family settlement applications, including spouse or partner visas.

- **Structure**: <u>The form is 18 pages long and consists of several parts</u>.

    o **Part 1: Personal Details**: Information about the applicant, including name, date of birth, nationality, and passport details.

    o **Part 2: Relationship to Sponsor**: Details about your relationship with your partner, including how you met, how long you have been together, and any previous marriages or civil partnerships.

    o **Part 3: Accommodation Details**: Information about where you will live in the UK, including the type of accommodation and whether it is owned or rented.

    o **Part 4: Financial Requirements**: Details about your financial situation, including income, savings, and employment.

- **Part 5: Additional Information**: Any other relevant information that supports your application.

Supporting Documents

- **Uploading Documents**: During the online application process, you will be prompted to upload supporting documents. Ensure all documents are clear and legible.

- **Document Checklist**: The UKVI website provides a checklist of required documents to help you ensure you have everything needed.

Guidance Notes

- **Reading Guidance**: Before completing the form, read the guidance notes provided by UKVI. <u>These notes offer detailed instructions on how to fill out each section of the form and what information is required</u>

- **Submission**

- **Review**: Carefully review your application before submitting it to ensure all information is accurate and complete.

- **Payment**: Pay the application fee and the Immigration Health Surcharge (IHS) as part of the submission process.

- **Confirmation**: After submission, you will receive a confirmation email with details on the next steps, including biometric information submission and any required interviews.

These details should help you understand the process of completing the application form for a UK spouse or partner visa

6 BIOMETRIC INFORMATION

What is Biometric Information?

Biometric information includes:

- **Fingerprints**: Scanned electronically.

- **Digital Photograph**: A photo of your face taken at the visa application center.

Why is it Required?

Biometric information is used to:

- Verify your identity.

- Issue a Biometric Residence Permit (BRP), which serves as proof of your right to stay in the UK.

Where to Provide Biometric Information

- **Outside the UK**: You will need to visit a visa application center in your country of residence.

- <u>**Inside the UK**: You can provide biometric information at a UK Visa and Citizenship Application Services (UKVCAS) service point or a Service and Support Centre (SSC)</u>

Steps to Provide Biometric Information

1. **Book an Appointment**: After submitting your online application, you will be prompted to book an appointment at a visa application center.

2. **Attend the Appointment**: Bring your passport and appointment confirmation. The process typically takes less than 5 minutes.

3. **Fingerprints**: Place your fingers on a glass screen to be scanned. This is a clean and quick process.

4. **Digital Photograph**: A digital photo of your face will be taken. You do not need to remove head coverings worn for religious or medical reasons.

5. **Children**: Children under 16 must be accompanied by a parent or guardian. <u>Children under 5 do not need to provide fingerprints</u>.

After Providing Biometric Information

- **Biometric Residence Permit (BRP)**: If your visa application is approved, you will receive a BRP. This card contains your biometric information and details about your visa status.

- **Collection**: If you applied from outside the UK, you must collect your BRP within 10 days of arriving in the UK.

Special Cases

- **Physical Inability**: If you are physically unable to provide fingerprints, only a digital photo will be taken. <u>This will be noted in your records</u>.

These details should help you understand the process of providing biometric information for a UK spouse or partner visa.

7 SUPPORTING DOCUMENTS

Here are more detailed explanations for each of the required supporting documents for a UK spouse or partner visa:

1. Passport

- **Applicant's Passport**: A valid passport or travel document for your partner. This should be current and have at least one blank page for the visa vignette.

- **Sponsor's Passport**: A copy of your passport or travel document to prove your British citizenship or settled status.

2. Proof of Relationship

- **Marriage or Civil Partnership Certificate**: If you are married or in a civil partnership, provide the official certificate.

- **Evidence of Living Together**: If you are not married but have lived together for at least 2 years, provide documents such as:

    - Joint tenancy agreements or mortgage statements.

    - Utility bills or council tax bills in both names.

    - Joint bank account statements.

    - <u>Correspondence addressed to both partners at the same address over the 2-year period</u>.

3. Financial Evidence

- **Payslips**: Typically, 6 months of payslips from your employment.

- **Bank Statements**: Corresponding bank statements showing the income being deposited.

- **Employment Letter**: A letter from your employer confirming your job, salary, and length of employment.

- **Self-Employment Documents**: If self-employed, provide recent tax returns, business accounts, and an accountant's letter.

- <u>**Savings**: If using savings to meet the financial requirement, provide bank statements showing the savings have been held for at least 6 months</u>.

   4. **Proof of Accommodation in the UK**

- **Tenancy Agreement or Mortgage Statement**: Proof of where you will live in the UK. This can be a rental agreement, mortgage statement, or a letter from family or friends confirming you can stay with them.

- **Property Inspection Report**: Sometimes required to show that the accommodation is adequate and not overcrowded.

   5. **English Language Proficiency Test Results (if applicable)**

- **Approved English Language Test Certificate**: If your partner needs to prove their knowledge of English, provide the test certificate from an approved provider. The test must be at least level A1 on the CEFR scale.

- **Academic Qualifications**: If your partner has a degree taught in English, provide the degree certificate and a certificate from Ecctis (formerly UK NARIC) confirming the qualification is equivalent to a UK degree.

Additional Documents

- **TB Test Certificate**: If your partner is from a country where tuberculosis (TB) testing is required, provide a TB test certificate from an approved clinic.

- **Previous Immigration Documents**: If your partner has previously been in the UK, provide copies of any previous visas or residence permits.

Submission Process

- **Online Submission**: Upload scanned copies of all required documents during the online application process.

- **Mail Submission**: If required, mail the original documents to the appropriate address provided by UKVI. Ensure all documents are clear and legible.

These details should help you gather and submit all the necessary documents for a UK spouse or partner visa application.

8 THE INTERVIEW

Purpose of the Interview.

<u>The primary goal of the interview is to verify the genuineness of your relationship and ensure that the marriage or partnership is not solely for immigration purposes</u>. The interview helps the UK Visas and Immigration (UKVI) officials assess the credibility of your application.

When is an Interview Required?

An interview may be required if:

- There are inconsistencies or gaps in your application or supporting documents.

- The caseworker needs further clarification

on certain aspects of your relationship.

- There are concerns about the authenticity of your relationship, such as a quick proposal or previous visa refusals.

Preparing for the Interview

- **Review Your Application**: Go through your application and supporting documents to ensure you are familiar with all the details.

   Practice Common Questions: Prepare for questions about your relationship, such as how you met, your daily routines, and future plans. Practicing with a friend or family member can help.

- **Gather Additional Documents**: Bring copies of all submitted documents and any new evidence that supports your application. This can include recent photos, communication records, and travel itineraries.

Common Interview Questions

You may be asked questions such as:

- How did you meet your spouse/partner?

- When and where did you get married or start living together?

- How do you communicate with each other?

- What are your spouse's/partner's hobbies and interests.

- <u>Have you met each other's families and friends?</u>

During the Interview

- **Stay Calm and Honest**: Answer questions truthfully and confidently. It's normal to feel nervous, but staying calm will help you provide clear and accurate answers.

- **Provide Detailed Answers**: Be specific in your responses. Avoid giving vague or one-word answers.

- **Bring Required Documents**: Ensure you have all necessary documents with you, including your passport, proof of relationship, and any additional evidence.

After the Interview

- **Decision**: The caseworker will review your interview responses along with your application and supporting documents. You will be notified of the decision in due course.

- **Follow-Up**: If additional information is needed, you may be contacted for further clarification or asked to provide more documents.

These details should help you prepare for and understand the interview process for a UK spouse or partner visa.

9 WAITING FOR A DECISION

Processing Times

- **Outside the UK**: The standard processing time for a spouse or partner visa application made from outside the UK is typically **2-3 months**.

- **Inside the UK**: If applying from within the UK, the processing time is usually **6-8 weeks**.

- **Extended Processing**: In some cases, processing may take longer if additional information or documents are required, or if an interview is needed.

Tracking Your Application

- **Online Tracking**: You can track the status of your application online through the UK Visas and Immigration (UKVI) website. You will need your application reference number to check the status.

- **Notifications**: You will receive email updates regarding the progress of your application. Once a decision is made, you will be notified by email or letter.

Receiving the Decision

- **Decision Letter**: You will receive a letter or email informing you of the decision on your visa application. This will include instructions on the next steps.

- **Vignette**: If your application is approved, your partner will receive a vignette (sticker) in their passport. This vignette allows them to travel to and enter the UK.

- **Biometric Residence Permit (BRP)**: Once in the UK, your partner will need to collect their BRP. The BRP is a physical card that confirms their identity and immigration status.

Collecting the BRP

- **Collection Point**: The decision letter will specify where to collect the BRP, usually from a designated Post Office branch or your sponsor's address if chosen during the application.

- **Timeframe**: Your partner must collect their BRP within 10 days of arriving in the UK or before the vignette expires, whichever is later.

- **Required Documents**: To collect the BRP, your partner will need to bring their passport with the vignette and the decision letterhttps://www.gov.uk/biometric-residence-permits/getting-your-brp-if-you-applied-from-outside-the-uk.

Possible Delays

- **Additional Checks**: Processing may take longer if further checks are needed, such as verifying documents or conducting an interview.

- **High Demand**: During peak times, such as

holidays or high application periods, processing times may be extended.

These details should help you understand the process of waiting for a decision on a UK spouse or partner visa and what to expect once a decision is made.

10 TRAVEL TO UK AND COLLECT BRP

Travel to the UK

Preparing for Travel

- **Documents to Carry**: Ensure your partner carries all relevant documents, including:

    o   Passport with the visa vignette.

    o   Decision letter from UKVI.

    o   Copies of the application and supporting documents.

    o   Proof of relationship and accommodation.

- Any additional documents that might be requested at the border.

Entering the UK

- **Arrival**: Upon arrival in the UK, your partner will need to present their passport with the visa vignette to the border control officer.

- **Border Control**: The officer may ask questions about the purpose of the visit and check the supporting documents. It's important to answer honestly and provide any requested documents.

- **Initial Entry**: The vignette allows entry into the UK for a specified period (usually 30 or 90 days). During this time, your partner must collect their Biometric Residence Permit (BRP).

11. Collect the BRP

What is a BRP?

- **Biometric Residence Permit (BRP)**: A BRP is a card that contains your partner's biometric information (fingerprints and photo) and details about their immigration status. It serves as proof of their right to stay in the UK.

Collection Process

- **Timeframe**: Your partner must collect their BRP within 10 days of arriving in the UK or before the vignette expires, whichever is later.

- **Collection Point**: The decision letter will specify where to collect the BRP, usually from a designated Post Office branch or your sponsor's address if chosen during the application.

- **Required Documents**: To collect the BRP, your partner will need to bring:

    o Passport with the visa vignette.

    o Decision letter from UKVI.

Steps to Collect the BRP

1. **Locate the Collection Point**: Check the decision letter for the specified Post Office branch or sponsor's address.

2. **Visit the Collection Point**: Go to the designated location within the specified timeframe.

3. **Present Documents**: Show the passport with the vignette and the decision letter to the staff at the collection point.

4. **Receive the BRP**: The staff will verify the documents and hand over the BRP.

Important Considerations

- **Failure to Collect**: If your partner does not collect the BRP within the specified timeframe, they may face penalties or issues with their immigration status.

- **Leaving and Re-entering the UK**: If your partner needs to leave and re-enter the UK before collecting the BRP, they must apply for a 'replacement BRP visa' to re-enter the UK.

These details should help you understand the process of traveling to the UK and collecting the BRP.

Visit Arthurcrandon.co.uk for More Titles

Retirement to the Philippines
K1 Fiance visa to the U.S. – Fast Track
Secrets to buying Condos in the Philippines
Buying Land in the Philippines
Annulment in the Philippines
Breaking free from a bad marriage
Get a visit visa to America First time
Marriage in the Philippines
Get a visit visa to the United Kingdom
Ghosts, Spectres, and folklore in the Philippines
Retiring to Spain – a Comprehensive Guide
Spousal Visa to America
Spousal visa to the United Kingdom

ABOUT THE AUTHOR

Arthur Crandon is a retired lawyer and a prolific writer. Hi is British and grew up in a rural community in Somerset. He has lived in England, Wales, Hong Kong and the Philippines and now spends most of his time in the Philippines with his Visayan wife and their son.

He loves to hear from anyone who has anything to do with the Philippines – you can email him anytime on:

ac@arthurcrandon.co.uk

www.ingramcontent.com/pod-product-compliance
Lightning Source LLC
Chambersburg PA
CBHW030051230526
45471CB00003B/1043